CW01465309

Original title:
Insightful Unions

Author: Liisu Laulurind
ISBN HARDBACK: 978-9916-87-243-7
ISBN PAPERBACK: 978-9916-87-244-4
ISBN EBOOK: 978-9916-87-245-1

A Universe of Us

In the quiet night we dwell,
Stars whisper secrets they can't tell.
Galaxy spins in a dance of light,
Our dreams ignite in the soft twilight.

Together we sail on cosmic streams,
Chasing the echoes of fading dreams.
Planets collide, yet we remain,
In the warmth of love, we feel no pain.

Infinite wonders lie in our sight,
Every heartbeat is pure delight.
Nebulas swirl with colors bright,
Illuminating paths in the dark of night.

With every glance, the universe glows,
A bond unbroken as time surely flows.
In this vast expanse, it's clear to see,
A universe of us, just you and me.

The Art of Together

In all the colors that we blend,
A canvas grows with every hand.
Brushstrokes meet where hearts extend,
Creating visions, grand and planned.

With laughter, tears, and fleeting grace,
We weave a story rich and bright.
Together, find a sacred space,
Where dreams take flight, igniting light.

Between Us, a Universe

In whispers soft, the stars align,
Two souls connect, an endless dance.
The cosmos swirls in every sign,
A journey sparked by fated chance.

Within the silence, worlds are born,
A galaxy of thoughts declared.
No space too vast, no bond forlorn,
In unity, our hearts are bared.

Light and Shadow Entwined

In every shadow, light will peek,
A gentle glow, a fleeting spark.
Together, both create the peak,
Of beauty found within the dark.

Embrace the dusk, then greet the dawn,
For every shade holds grace and hope.
In balance, life weaves on and on,
In harmony, we learn to cope.

Unity in Diversity

In every voice, a song is sung,
A tapestry of tales we weave.
Each note a gift, both old and young,
We gather strength, together believe.

From every heart, a different beat,
Our differences, a vibrant hue.
In tandem, we turn struggles sweet,
Unity found, where love breaks through.

Points of Convergence

In shadows where we meet,
A blend of dreams we greet.
Paths woven fine and neat,
Whispers in the heartbeat.

Strangers in the night,
Our stories take their flight.
Across the starry light,
Together, we ignite.

Beyond the Horizon Together

We chase the glowing dawn,
Where weary hearts belong.
Hand in hand, we move on,
With strength that feels so strong.

Mountains rise and fall,
Through valleys, we will crawl.
United through it all,
Our spirits hear the call.

A Chorus of Souls

Voices blend in the air,
Each note beyond compare.
Together, we will share,
A harmony, so rare.

In laughter and in tears,
We echo through the years.
Resounding through our fears,
Our song softly clears.

Ways of Knowing Each Other

In silence, eyes convey,
Thoughts tethered in the sway.
Understanding finds a way,
Through gestures as we play.

A smile, a gentle nod,
Moments that feel like God.
In simple acts, we trod,
Creating paths we laud.

The Embrace of Kinship

In a circle of laughter we dwell,
Hearts entwined, where warm stories swell.
Through trials faced, our spirits rise,
In every hug, a love that ties.

Together we journey, side by side,
In the tapestry of life, we confide.
Roots run deep, like an ancient tree,
Bound by affection, forever free.

Finding Common Ground

Two paths collide in twilight's glow,
In shared moments, understanding flows.
Hand in hand, we pave the way,
Building bridges, come what may.

Voices blend in harmony sweet,
Diverse melodies in a dance so neat.
Unity found beneath the stars,
Together we rise, no more wars.

The Light Between Us

In silence shared, a tranquil spark,
Guides us gently, through the dark.
Illuminated by dreams we share,
In the shadows, we find our care.

A flicker of hope, a guiding flame,
In this journey, we're never the same.
With every step, our spirits twine,
In the light of love, our souls align.

Threads of Shared Stories

Woven tales of joy and strife,
Each thread a piece of our shared life.
In whispered words, our dreams take flight,
Together we soar into the night.

Every chapter holds a lesson dear,
In tales of laughter, we shed a tear.
With every stitch, our bond grows strong,
In the fabric of time, we all belong.

The Language of Shared Experience

In laughter and tears, stories unfold,
Moments like threads, in tapestry gold.
Voices unite, in harmony find,
A language of hearts, beautifully kind.

With every embrace, a lesson is learned,
The fire of friendship, forever burned.
In silence we speak, in glances we see,
A world intertwined, just you and me.

Hidden Treasures of Alliance

Beneath the surface, gems lie in wait,
In bonds we discover, a shimmering fate.
Together we dig, through layers so deep,
The treasures of trust, in our hearts we keep.

In laughter shared, and challenges faced,
The wealth of our union, never replaced.
With each whispered secret, a promise we find,
Hidden treasures ever, in love intertwined.

Crossing Bridges Together

On paths we traverse, through valleys and hills,
With courage as compass, and faith that fulfills.
Hand in hand we wander, we make our own way,
Together we thrive, come what may.

Each bridge that we cross, a story we weave,
In moments of doubt, it's hope we believe.
For it's not just the journey, but who by our side,
In union we flourish, our hearts open wide.

The Weaving of Souls

Threads of connection, interlaced tight,
In shadows and sunlight, we spark pure delight.
With each passing moment, our patterns unfold,
A tapestry vibrant, with stories retold.

In the loom of our lives, we craft with great care,
Each knot a reminder, that love we will share.
With colors of laughter, and shades of our pain,
The weaving of souls, forever will reign.

The Bridge of Understanding

In whispers soft, we share our thoughts,
Beneath the stars, where silence knots.
Two worlds collide, find common ground,
In every heart, a truth is found.

With open minds, we seek to learn,
Each tale unfolds, a chance to turn.
Though paths diverge, our spirits soar,
On this bridge, we find much more.

Luminescence of Together

Underneath the glowing skies,
Together we stand, where solace lies.
With every laugh, our spirits blaze,
In unity, we set the praise.

Through darkened nights, we find our way,
Guided by hope, forever stay.
In every challenge, hand in hand,
We shine as one, a radiant band.

The Weight of Shared Dreams

In whispered hopes, we lift the load,
A journey paved, the heart's abode.
With every step, our visions blend,
Together strong, we shall transcend.

Through valleys low and mountains high,
We chase the stars, we touch the sky.
In unity, our dreams take flight,
With every heartbeat, pure delight.

Symphony of Differences

In colors bright, our stories sing,
Each note distinct, yet harmonizing.
With every voice, a melody,
In this grand dance, we find the key.

Though varied paths, we share the stage,
In life's great play, we turn the page.
Diverse and bold, we weave our fate,
A symphony that we create.

Radiance of Companionship

In the glow of shared laughter,
Under the canvas of twilight,
Two souls dance in connection,
Creating warmth, pure and bright.

A gentle touch speaks volumes,
Every glance, a silent song,
In the tapestry of friendship,
We find where we belong.

Through the storms and the sunshine,
We stand strong side by side,
In the heart of companionship,
A radiant love, our guide.

With every step together,
Our spirits weave a thread,
In the embrace of companionship,
Endless joy lies ahead.

Unspoken Affinities

Between the words we never say,
Lies a bond, deep and true,
In silent sighs and fleeting glances,
My heart speaks only to you.

The whispers of the evening breeze,
Carry secrets of our souls,
In the dance of our quiet moments,
A connection that consoles.

Two minds entwined in stillness,
Finding solace in the night,
In unspoken affinities,
Our spirits take their flight.

A language formed in silence,
A bond that needs no sound,
In the depths of understanding,
A love profoundly found.

Intertwined Journeys

Paths that cross under starlit skies,
Winding tales of fate unfurl,
Together we roam through the unknown,
In this vast and wondrous world.

Every twist brings new adventure,
Hand in hand, we face the fears,
In the rhythm of our journeys,
We gather laughter, shed our tears.

With each step, old dreams revive,
As new horizons come to view,
In the dance of our journeys,
Forever I walk with you.

No map needed for this venture,
In each heartbeat, we discover,
In the intertwining of our paths,
A bond that can't be smothered.

The Poetry of Connection

In the verses of our laughter,
Every moment, a soft rhyme,
Painting memories with colors,
Etched in the sands of time.

A sonnet penned in whispers,
Echoing through the air,
In the poetry of connection,
We find solace, unaware.

Each heartbeat, a stanza written,
In the book of you and me,
In the rhythm, we find meaning,
In the flow, we're truly free.

With every line, our story grows,
In a dance of give and take,
In the poetry of connection,
Together we awaken.

The Dance of Two Souls

In the moonlight's soft embrace,
Two souls sway with gentle grace.
Their whispers echo through the night,
In a world that feels so right.

With every turn, they intertwine,
Rhythms match, their hearts align.
A melody of love takes flight,
In a dance that feels so bright.

Through every laugh, through every tear,
They find solace, always near.
Together they step, side by side,
In this dance, they will abide.

As dawn breaks, their shadows fade,
Yet the memories serenade.
With each heartbeat, they will know,
The dance of souls will ever grow.

Tapestry of Emotions

In colors rich and threads so bold,
Stories of love and pain unfold.
With each stitch, a moment's grace,
A tapestry of life we trace.

Joy and sorrow weave a blend,
In tight embrace, they softly mend.
A vibrant quilt, both dark and light,
Reflecting hearts in day and night.

The fibers sing a silent tune,
Beneath the sun, beneath the moon.
Woven dreams and memories call,
In this tapestry, we find all.

Through every fray, through every tear,
The shadows linger, yet we bear.
With every hue, we feel the sway,
In this tapestry, we find our way.

Unveiling Hidden Harmonies

In silence deep, the echoes wait,
Secrets poised to captivate.
Notes untold, in whispers blend,
Harmony begins to extend.

With gentle hands, we lift the veil,
Revealing sounds like a sweet trail.
The melodies, once kept apart,
Now dance, igniting every heart.

Through tender notes, we learn to see,
The beauty found in mystery.
In every chord, new worlds arise,
Unveiling truth beneath the skies.

As symphonies begin to soar,
We'll find the magic at the core.
Together, we'll explore the space,
Unveiling harmonies with grace.

The Meeting of Minds

In quiet corners, thoughts converge,
A spark ignites, ideas surge.
Two minds collide in radiant light,
Creating worlds of sheer delight.

Questions flow like rivers wide,
In the midst, they seek and bide.
What if's linger in the air,
Fueling dreams that dare to share.

With every thought, a bridge is built,
Connecting souls without the guilt.
In conversation's sweet embrace,
A meeting found in timeless space.

As visions merge and pathways blend,
New beginnings bloom and mend.
Together, they craft a grand design,
In the meeting of their minds.

In Harmony We Stand

In whispers of the gentle breeze,
We gather strength from rooted trees.
Each voice a note, a part of song,
Together, we know we belong.

With every step, a path we pave,
The bonds we forge, the hearts we save.
In unity, our spirits rise,
We find our peace beneath the skies.

In the stillness of the night,
We share our dreams, a guiding light.
With hands entwined, we face the storm,
In harmony, our hearts feel warm.

As dawn breaks, a tapestry,
Woven from our shared history.
Together we stand, side by side,
In harmony, no need to hide.

Paths of Mutual Growth

Through winding roads, we find our way,
In each spoken word, there's room to sway.
With open hearts, we learn to see,
The strength that blooms from you and me.

In shared laughter and gentle tears,
We nurture trust and conquer fears.
Together we plant the seeds of care,
In the garden of hope, we lay them bare.

Each stumble leads to lessons found,
In every silence, love is profound.
With every challenge that we face,
We grow in strength, we find our place.

Guided by the stars above,
We cultivate a world of love.
On paths we walk, both near and far,
Together, we shine like distant stars.

Reflections in Each Other

In your eyes, I see my truth,
A mirror showing measured youth.
With every glance, our souls ignite,
In reflections soft, we find our light.

Through trials faced, we hold a space,
For all the dreams that we embrace.
In every laughter, every sigh,
Reflections dance, they never lie.

The stories shared, our hearts unfold,
In whispered tales of brave and bold.
Together in silence, we find peace,
In the depths of love, our fears decrease.

As we navigate this winding road,
Our bond creates a loving code.
In reflections deep, forever clear,
Together always, I hold you near.

Nature of Togetherness

In the rustling leaves, we hear the call,
A gentle reminder, we are one and all.
With every heartbeat, nature sings,
The beauty found in simple things.

With seasons changing, hand in hand,
We learn to flourish, to understand.
Through storms that come and sunsets glow,
Together, we thrive, we learn to grow.

In the colors of the evening sky,
We find our solace, you and I.
In nature's arms, we take our stand,
United here, a promised land.

In every petal, every tree,
Together, we find harmony.
The nature of love, forever true,
In togetherness, I find you.

Shared Horizons

Golden fields stretch wide and far,
Beneath the vast, unending sky.
Hearts united, we chase the star,
Finding solace where dreams lie.

Whispers of wind tell tales anew,
In the twilight's gentle embrace.
Together, we share each view,
Hand in hand, we find our place.

Mountains loom, majestic and grand,
Rivers dance, joyfully they flow.
With every step, we make our stand,
Creating memories as we grow.

In shared horizons, hope ignites,
A tapestry of warmth and light.
With open hearts, we soar to heights,
In unity, our spirits bright.

Where Paths Entwine

Two roads converge in morning's glow,
Footsteps echo, side by side.
In every laughter, seeds we sow,
Beneath the sky, our dreams abide.

Fate weaves threads of joy and chance,
As we navigate this winding trail.
With every heartbeat, we advance,
Love's gentle map will never fail.

Moments blend, like colors bright,
Painting scenes of our shared quest.
In shadows cast by fading light,
We find our rhythm, we find rest.

Together we wander, hand in hand,
Through valleys deep and mountains tall.
In every challenge, we make a stand,
In this sweet journey, we have it all.

The Circle of Trust

Gathered round in whispered tones,
A bond we craft with every gaze.
In safe embrace, we lay our bones,
A sanctuary, our hearts ablaze.

Knowing looks, no words required,
Each heartbeat sings a melody.
In the silence, love's spark is fired,
Together, we are wild and free.

Through laughter shared and tears that fall,
We weave our stories, thread by thread.
In the circle, we give our all,
In every word, our souls are fed.

Trust envelops like morning dew,
A soft caress, a gentle breath.
In every moment, we renew,
This bond unbroken, conquering death.

The Embrace of Contrasts

Day meets night in a vibrant dance,
Colors clash, yet find their way.
In every glance, there's a chance,
To learn from shadows, in the fray.

Sweet and bitter, laughter and sighs,
Life's tapestry, rich and complex.
Through stormy skies and clear blue highs,
We find our path amidst the wrecks.

Fire and ice, they intertwine,
Bringing balance to all we know.
With every moment, a chance to shine,
Through diverse paths, together we grow.

In contrast's arms, we learn to stand,
Embracing both light and dark's sway.
United in love, hand in hand,
We revel in what life's shades convey.

The Alchemy of Us

In shadows deep, we find our light,
Together forging, day and night.
With hearts aligned, we shape our fate,
A bond of gold, it won't abate.

Through trials faced, we break the mold,
In unity, our story's told.
Each challenge met, our spirits rise,
With every step, a new surprise.

Beneath the Surface of Us

In quiet depths, our secrets dwell,
A world unseen, where whispers swell.
Through currents strong, we find our place,
In every glance, a soft embrace.

With roots entwined, we grow as one,
In silence shared, our journey's begun.
Each layer peeled, a treasure's revealed,
Beneath the waves, our truths are sealed.

Hands Joined in Purpose

With hands held tight, we face the storm,
Together strong, we break the norm.
Through every strife, our spirits soar,
In unity, we seek for more.

Each heart a beat, in perfect time,
Our voices rise, in hope they chime.
Bound by a dream, we dare to strive,
With courage found, we truly thrive.

The Colors of Cooperation

In every hue, our strengths combine,
A canvas bright, our fates entwine.
With brush in hand, we paint the scene,
In harmony, we craft the dream.

Each tone a note, in perfect tune,
Together we will reach for the moon.
Through every shade, our story spreads,
In vibrant threads, our vision treads.

Unexpected Alignments

In the stillness, stars collide,
Silent forces, side by side,
Paths converge, none can foresee,
In the chaos, harmony.

With each moment, fate unspins,
Secrets hidden, light begins,
Tangled threads find their own way,
In the night, they softly play.

Echoes linger, shadows waltz,
Destinies entwined in faults,
Wonders woven, grace in chance,
In the darkness, stars shall dance.

Unexpected, yet so divine,
In the still, a sacred sign,
Leading hearts to find their song,
In the quiet, we belong.

Heartbeats in Synchrony

Two souls tethered, pulse aligned,
In the silence, love defined,
Rhythms echo, soft and clear,
In each heartbeat, draw you near.

Moments captured, breaths in sync,
In the still, we stop to think,
Every glance, a silent vow,
Time stands still, this is our now.

Waves of warmth, a gentle swell,
In your eyes, a secret spell,
Together, we embrace the flow,
In the dance, our spirits glow.

With each thump, we rise and fall,
In this world, you are my call,
Heartbeats whisper, sweet as wine,
In this sync, our love will shine.

A Canvas of Collaboration

Brushstrokes mingle, colors blend,
In creation, hearts transcend,
Every shade, a story told,
In this union, dreams unfold.

Hands together, visions rise,
Underneath a painted sky,
Layered hopes, we spin the thread,
In the art, our souls are fed.

Textures weave, the canvas breathes,
In this space, the heart believes,
Crafted moments, bold and bright,
In this dance, we find our light.

Brush and pen, the tools we choose,
In collaboration, we won't lose,
With every stroke, creation sings,
In this canvas, love takes wings.

Resonating Whispers

In a breeze, soft words escape,
Secrets linger, hearts reshape,
Whispers echo, gentle tones,
In our silence, love atones.

Fleeting moments, shared as one,
Underneath the fading sun,
Tender glances, soft and shy,
In the night, our dreams will fly.

Threads of sound, a calming breeze,
In our minds, the stirring seas,
Every whisper finds its way,
In the dark, our hopes convey.

Resonating, shadows play,
In each heartbeat, night and day,
Through the quiet, love will stir,
In these echoes, we confer.

A Nexus of Voices

In the heart of silence, echoes ring,
Many tales of longing, waiting to sing.
Whispers of wisdom, ancient and new,
Gathered together, in vibrant hue.

Each voice a thread, in a woven seam,
Stories intertwined, like a shared dream.
Harmony rises, in dialogue's grace,
Finding our truth, in this sacred space.

A Journey of Many Steps

Each step we take, on paths unknown,
With every stumble, we've brightly grown.
Footprints behind, like tales in the sand,
Marking our journey, where dreams expand.

The road may twist, and rivers may bend,
Yet onward we march, with hearts to mend.
Hand in hand, with purpose in stride,
Together we'll face the rising tide.

Discovering Unity

In the garden of voices, we plant the seeds,
Diverse and unique, each one leads.
Flowers of thought, in colors unite,
Blooming together, in fragrant delight.

Reaching for bonds, that hold us as one,
Shadows and light, under the sun.
Finding connection, through laughter and tears,
Building a future, that dispels our fears.

A Palette of Perspectives

Brushstrokes of thought, vivid and bright,
Each color a tale, in day or night.
From shadows of doubt, to the light of dreams,
Art of expression, is more than it seems.

A canvas of minds, where ideas blend,
Creating a picture, that knows no end.
In the swirl of opinions, we find our place,
A masterpiece crafted, with love and grace.

When Paths Collide in Radiance

Two souls meet where shadows play,
In the light of a dawning day.
With laughter shared and dreams unfold,
In that moment, love takes hold.

Each step ignites a spark so bright,
Guiding hearts through the night.
In the dance of fate's gentle hands,
Together they weave their plans.

Through swirling stars, their laughter flows,
Bridging the gap where courage grows.
In silence, whispers dwell and rise,
As truth shines clear in their eyes.

Infinite paths aligned above,
In chaos, they find their love.
Through the maze of choice and chance,
Eternal is this radiant dance.

The Convergence of Inner Worlds

In the depths of every heart,
Two worlds collide, never apart.
Moments shared with gentle grace,
In the stillness, they find their space.

Echoes of thoughts intertwine,
In the silence, their souls shine.
Through whispered dreams, they connect,
In the shadows, hearts reflect.

Beyond borders, they find their way,
In every word, a chance to play.
The tapestry of dreams takes flight,
Illuminating paths of light.

With every heartbeat, stories weave,
In the quiet, they learn to believe.
Two worlds blending, side by side,
In this union, they confide.

Whispers of Connection

In the stillness of a gentle breeze,
Voices softly float with ease.
Threads of kindness, woven tight,
Embrace the darkness, bring in light.

With every glance, a story told,
In shared moments, hearts unfold.
Through laughter, tears, and sweet surprise,
The whispers guide, the spirit flies.

In crowded rooms yet still alone,
Find the comfort, find the home.
Through fleeting time, a bond is born,
In quiet strength, they are reborn.

Like raindrops on a sunlit stream,
Together, they dance, they dream.
In connection, silent and true,
The world awakens, anew for two.

Threads of Understanding

In the fabric of life's design,
Each thread a story intertwined.
With every knot, a lesson learned,
In gentle hands, the heart is turned.

Patterns shifting, colors blend,
In the tapestry, we find a friend.
Through bonds that stretch yet never break,
With every laugh, the soul awakes.

In the warmth of a knowing glance,
Through the struggles, we dare to dance.
In shared struggles, laughter and tears,
Unity flourishes, easing fears.

Understanding blooms like springtime's grace,
In the moments where we embrace.
Through the fibers, hearts remain,
In every thread, love's refrain.

Affinity at Dawn

In the morning light so pure,
Silent whispers start to stir.
Hearts entwined, they feel the glow,
As the world begins to grow.

Gentle breezes cross the way,
Carrying dreams of the day.
In this moment, they are one,
Underneath the rising sun.

Every step, a dance of grace,
Time slows down in this sweet space.
Life awakens with the morn,
In their souls, a bond is sworn.

With each heartbeat, hope takes flight,
Guided by love's tender light.
In the dawn, they find their place,
Launching forth in warm embrace.

Mosaics of Belonging

Pieces scattered far and wide,
Yet together, they abide.
Colors bright and shades beyond,
In their hearts, a common bond.

Every fragment tells a tale,
Of journeys taken, hearts that sail.
In each story, truth resounds,
In this maze, a love surrounds.

Different paths, yet dreams align,
Building bridges intertwined.
Hand in hand, they weave and stitch,
Creating life, a seamless pitch.

Each mosaic, fresh and new,
A tapestry of me and you.
In the art where we belong,
Echoes of our shared song.

A Horizon of Connections

Beneath the sky, the world expands,
Where hopes and dreams make steady stands.
Eyes meet in the glowing light,
A spectrum of paths, shining bright.

Across the distance, hearts can feel,
The strength of bonds that slowly heal.
Every wave and every sound,
A tapestry of love is found.

When shadows stretch and daylight fades,
The horizon gleams with promises made.
Together, they chase the sun,
In this journey, they are one.

With open hearts, they face the day,
Through every challenge, come what may.
As connections blend and grow,
There's beauty in what we sow.

The Pulse of Partnership

In the rhythm of each beat,
Two souls dance on life's warm street.
Hand in hand, they face the night,
Together, they are filled with light.

With every laugh, the world expands,
In silent trust, they take their stands.
Through every trial, they will cope,
Bound by the threads of endless hope.

In the stillness, whispers speak,
A language soft, a bond unique.
Two hearts beating as one sound,
In this unity, love is found.

In every echo, dreams resound,
With every moment, joy is crowned.
Through life's pulse, they'll find their way,
In partnership, come what may.

When Hearts Collide

In a crowded room, our eyes meet,
A spark ignites, both wild and sweet.
Whispers dance, the air feels warm,
Two lives entwined, a perfect storm.

Every heartbeat synchronizes,
In this moment, love arises.
Time suspends, the world fades away,
When hearts collide, come what may.

Amidst the chaos, you find my hand,
Together we soar, together we stand.
With every look, we share a truth,
In this collision, lies eternal youth.

As shadows wane and daylight breaks,
The magic of us, in every ache.
When hearts collide, they find their way,
A beautiful mess, forever we stay.

Echoes of Togetherness

In quiet moments filled with grace,
I hear your laughter, a warm embrace.
Soft whispers linger in the night,
Echoes of us, holding on tight.

Every shared secret, every glance,
A symphony of a timeless dance.
The world outside may roar and shout,
But in our hearts, there's never doubt.

Memories weave like threads of gold,
Stories of courage, together we hold.
In the silence, our souls entwine,
Echoes of love, forever divine.

With every challenge, side by side,
In the journey, our spirits abide.
Together we flourish, not just survive,
In this harmony, we truly thrive.

Bonds Beyond Words

In glances shared, a tale unfolds,
A narrative written in love's molds.
No need for speech, our hearts convey,
Bonds beyond words, come what may.

Through trials faced, we stand as one,
Underneath the vast, shining sun.
In silence, we find a sacred space,
Connection deep, time can't erase.

Every heartbeat, a rhythmic song,
In this togetherness, we belong.
Our laughter echoes through the years,
Bonded tightly, through joy and tears.

As seasons shift and ages grace,
We walk together, at our own pace.
Through every storm, our spirits soar,
Bonds beyond words, forevermore.

Harmony in Dissonance

In clashing tones, a song is born,
From chaos, beauty, to be adorned.
When voices rise and plans collide,
In this dissonance, we'll abide.

Amidst the noise, a truth we find,
Different paths, yet hearts combined.
In every clash, a lesson learned,
Through every bridge we've ever burned.

Conflict dances, yet love prevails,
Through stormy nights, we set our sails.
Finding balance, take my hand,
In harmony, we make our stand.

The world outside may seem askew,
But in our hearts, we see what's true.
In dissonance, a melody clear,
Together we rise, conquering fear.

Embracing Dual Realities

In the quiet of the night, shadows play,
Whispers of dreams dance under the moon's sway.
Two worlds collide, both soft and bright,
In paradox lies the heart of the light.

Time flows like water, endless and free,
Moments intertwine, you and me.
A tapestry woven of joy and strife,
Embracing the duality, we find our life.

Hope and despair, they walk hand in hand,
Building our castles on shifting sand.
In the embrace of both joy and sorrow,
We cherish today, we shape tomorrow.

Each heartbeat echoes a silent song,
In the balance of worlds, we all belong.
Together we stand, both fierce and mild,
In the dance of realities, the heart of a child.

Confluence of Thought and Feeling

Thoughts like rivers, they twist and turn,
Flowing through valleys where passions burn.
The heart beats softly, a gentle plea,
In the confluence, we find harmony.

Words may falter, yet feelings soar,
In the silence, our spirits explore.
A bridge of understanding, built with care,
In the space between, we lay ourselves bare.

When logic falters and emotions strike,
We seek the balance, a moment alike.
Two streams converge, rich and profound,
In the interplay, life's truth is found.

As the mind and heart begin to unite,
We find our way through the starry night.
Forging a path where love can thrive,
In the confluence, we learn to live.

The Language of Unity

Under the sky, where all hearts meet,
A language emerges, soft and sweet.
With every smile, a sentence is spun,
In the silence, two souls become one.

No need for words, just a knowing glance,
In shared moments, we find our chance.
Unity whispers in the light of the day,
In the bond we forge, we learn how to play.

Through laughter and tears, we weave our tale,
In every hardship, we set our sail.
From the depths of struggle, a chorus will rise,
In the language of love, no need for disguise.

Together we journey, through thick and thin,
In the heart of unity, we both shall win.
As one we stand, in joy and pain,
In the language of unity, we break every chain.

Interwoven Destinies

Fates like threads, intertwined and strong,
A tapestry woven, where we all belong.
Each life a pattern, intricate and bright,
In the fabric of time, we find our light.

With every choice, a stitch we create,
In the loom of existence, we navigate.
Through twists and turns, our paths align,
In the web of destinies, love will shine.

Moments converge, like rivers they flow,
Across the landscape of life, we grow.
In the dance of chance, we find our true call,
The interwoven destinies, connecting us all.

Together we rise, on this journey we tread,
With hope as our guide, no need for dread.
In the sacred threads that bind us so tight,
We embrace our fates, in the shared light.

Embracing Our Differences

In every hue, a story lies,
Threads of culture intertwine.
Voices rise, in harmony,
Celebrating what is divine.

Unity in every face,
Dancing to a varied tune.
Hearts that beat in swift embrace,
Underneath the same bright moon.

Let us weave a brighter tale,
With respect as our guiding star.
Together, we shall never fail,
Expanding love both near and far.

Difference is our strength relate,
In the dance of life's grand show.
Together we can cultivate,
Understanding's gentle flow.

In the Heart of Synergy

Two hands join in perfect grace,
Creating rhythms, bold and bright.
In the stillness, paths embrace,
Turning darkness into light.

With every step, we share a dream,
Where visions spark and hopes align.
In teamwork's pulse, we're more than team,
As one, we rise, together shine.

Bound by trust, we find our way,
Through challenges that test the heart.
With open minds, we dare to play,
Crafting futures, art by art.

Synergy blooms, a vibrant flower,
In the garden of our souls.
Together, we unleash the power,
Of unity, our shared goal.

secret paths converge

Whispers linger on the breeze,
Tales of journeys, hidden roads.
In the twilight, hearts find ease,
As the quiet mystery unfolds.

Here, where shadows dance and sway,
Footprints mark the earth beneath.
Hidden stories come to play,
Secrets spun with every breath.

Time circles round, a sacred loop,
Paths once distant now align.
In this sacred, endless group,
All our lives meet, intertwine.

Let the echoes softly sing,
As we walk this winding trail.
In the night, new dreams take wing,
Where our secret paths prevail.

Reflections of Duality

In the mirror, shadows blend,
Light and dark in close embrace.
Every story has an end,
Yet in beginnings, find your place.

Faces change but hearts remain,
Through the storms and sunny days.
In the joy, we feel the pain,
In the loss, life's tender ways.

Harmony from discord grows,
In every clash, a chance to see.
Duality, a gift bestows,
In the dance of you and me.

Celebrate what makes us whole,
A tapestry of every thread.
In the depths, we find our soul,
In the light, our fears are shed.

Serendipity in Union

In the stillness of the night,
Two hearts find their gentle light.
Fate weaves threads unseen,
Uniting souls, serene.

Moments born from chance's sway,
Guide us softly on our way.
In laughter and whispered dreams,
Life's magic flows in streams.

Paths converging, stars align,
In your eyes, my comfort shines.
Every glance, a spark divine,
Serendipity's sweet sign.

Hand in hand through time we roam,
In this journey, we create home.
With every breath, we intertwine,
Sweet serendipity, you are mine.

Hearts Entwined in Reflection

In the mirror of your gaze,
I see love's gentle haze.
Moments shared, a silent song,
Where the wildest dreams belong.

Time stands still, a sacred pause,
In every beat, life's tender cause.
Hearts entwined, a dance so pure,
In reflection, we find our cure.

With every tear, a lesson learned,
In every joy, the fire burned.
Together, shadows fade away,
In love's embrace, we choose to stay.

Two souls woven, side by side,
In this journey, we take pride.
Every thought, a shared connection,
In our hearts, a deep reflection.

The Map of Shared Journeys

Across the landscape of our days,
We chart our course in countless ways.
Each step forward, hand in hand,
Guided by dreams we understand.

With every mile, a story unfolds,
In the warmth of laughter, we are bold.
Unspoken bonds, a guiding star,
The map of love shows who we are.

Through valleys low and mountains high,
Side by side, we reach the sky.
With every twist, the path appears,
In shared journeys, we shed our fears.

Memories etched in twilight's glow,
In every heartbeat, love will grow.
Together, we navigate the night,
A map of journeys, pure and bright.

Rhythms of Compassionate Encounters

In the dance of fleeting time,
Compassion sings in every rhyme.
With every heartbeat, kindness flows,
In simple gestures, love bestows.

The world around us, vast and wide,
Yet here we stand, with hearts as guides.
In shared glances, a story told,
Rhythms of compassion, bold.

Through trials faced, we find our way,
In every challenge, brighter day.
In the embrace of understanding,
A world of warmth, expanding.

Every moment, a chance to share,
In the silence, we find our care.
With every smile, a bond that grows,
Rhythms of compassion, life bestows.

A Symphony of Intertwined Lives

In the hum of everyday sounds,
Hearts connect, their rhythm found.
Every glance a note in time,
Each smile a melody, pure and sublime.

When laughter echoes through the air,
It weaves a bond beyond compare.
In silence shared, in moments bright,
We craft our song in the soft twilight.

Together we dance in the twilight's glow,
A tapestry rich, with threads to sew.
In the symphony, we play our part,
Intertwined lives, a work of art.

As the day fades and shadows blend,
The music of souls shall never end.
In every heartbeat, a story twirls,
A symphony of intertwined worlds.

Threads of Love and Understanding

In the loom of life, threads weave tight,
Colors of love, both warm and bright.
Each stitch a moment, a memory shared,
Binding us closer, showing we cared.

Across the fabric, we gently tread,
With empathy woven, our fears shed.
In the tapestry of hope, hearts entwine,
Threads of understanding, a bond divine.

Through trials faced, together we stand,
For love, a thread, helps us withstand.
In storms and sunshine, we find our way,
With every weave, a promise to stay.

In the end, we see the grand design,
Through threads of love, our spirits align.
Each story unique, yet beautifully spun,
A masterpiece crafted, two souls as one.

The Art of Shared Solitude

In quiet corners, shadows play,
Solitude whispers, guiding the way.
In the stillness, hearts gently meet,
A canvas of silence, beautifully sweet.

Together we breathe, yet apart we stand,
In the space between, we understand.
With each quiet thought, a dialogue flows,
In the art of solitude, connection grows.

Moments linger, a serene embrace,
In shared stillness, we find our place.
With no words needed, souls can align,
In the gentle hush, our spirits entwine.

As the world spins, we cherish the pause,
Finding beauty in stillness, just because.
Each heartbeat echoes, a silent decree,
In the art of shared solitude, we are free.

Harmonious Convergences

Paths once separate now intertwine,
Under the stars, our fates align.
In moments brief, yet profoundly clear,
Harmonious convergences draw us near.

Life's gentle rhythm guides our way,
In serendipity, we find our play.
With open hearts, we ride the tide,
In unexpected meetings, love won't hide.

Along the journey, we share our dreams,
In echoes of laughter, joy redeems.
United in purpose, our spirits rise,
Harmonious convergences, a sweet surprise.

With every horizon, a chance to see,
The beauty in togetherness, bittersweet glee.
In this dance of life, we learn and grow,
Harmonious convergences, the heart's true glow.

Hearts in Silent Chorus

In the hush of night, they speak,
Whispers soft, voices meek.
Hearts entwined, in shadows dance,
Silent songs, deep in romance.

Underneath the silver moon,
Breathless tunes in quiet bloom.
Fingers brush, time holds its breath,
In this space, there lies no death.

Stars above, they weave their light,
Guiding souls through endless night.
Hearts in tune, they find their way,
In the chorus of the gray.

Through the stillness, love will rise,
Echoes sweet beneath the skies.
In this realm where silence reigns,
Hearts unite, shedding their chains.

Bridges of Empathy

Across the chasm, hearts do meet,
Building bridges, oh so sweet.
With open arms, they share their pain,
In understanding, love will reign.

Footsteps light on fragile lanes,
Each connection eases strains.
Voices blend in tender grace,
Offering solace in this space.

Waves of kindness, hands held tight,
Guiding through the darkest night.
With each word, a bond is formed,
Like a shelter, hearts transformed.

Together stronger, side by side,
Navigating with love as guide.
In our hearts, a light will spark,
Bridges built against the dark.

Bonds Beyond the Surface

In a glance, a truth unfolds,
Stories whispered, secrets told.
What lies deep beneath the skin,
Is where the journey must begin.

Beneath the laughter, pain resides,
Hidden tales, like ancient tides.
With each breath, we share our scars,
Mapping worlds, beneath the stars.

In the depths of knowing eyes,
Love transcends the thin disguise.
Finding warmth in our shared fears,
Crafting bonds that last through years.

Labelled surface, yet we dive,
In the deep, our spirits thrive.
Bonds that grow beyond the sphere,
In this space, we conquer fear.

Echoes of Connection

Whispers float on winds of change,
Carried far, yet not so strange.
In the silence, voices soar,
Echoes linger, forevermore.

Faint reminders of what's true,
Ties that bind me close to you.
In the dark, we find a spark,
A connection lights the dark.

Through the distance, hearts will call,
Reaching out, we will not fall.
In the pulse of life's embrace,
Echoes linger, time and space.

Every moment shapes our song,
In this chorus, we belong.
Though apart, together we stand,
Echoes woven, hand in hand.

Serenade of Kindred Minds

In the quiet of the night, they speak,
Whispers of dreams, gentle and meek.
Hearts in rhythm, like waves on shore,
Bound by thoughts that yearn for more.

Eyes that glimmer with secrets untold,
Stories of friendship, cherished and bold.
In laughter's echo, in silence's grace,
They find a haven, a sacred space.

With every word, they craft a song,
Voices united, where souls belong.
In the dance of thoughts, they twirl and spin,
A serenade of kindred minds within.

As stars align in the velvet sky,
Their spirits soar, learning to fly.
Across the cosmos, in twilight's gleam,
They weave their lives into a shared dream.

The Fabric of Togetherness

Threads intertwine in colors bright,
Woven hearts, a beautiful sight.
Each moment shared, a stitch in time,
Crafting a bond, a love sublime.

In laughter and tears, they find their way,
Building a tapestry, day by day.
Every memory, like pearls on a string,
Glistening what togetherness can bring.

In the warmth of a touch, in a knowing glance,
They dance to the rhythm of life's sweet chance.
Through storms and calm, they boldly stand,
United forever, hand in hand.

The fabric strong, stitched with care,
A quilt of moments, rich and rare.
In every thread, a story spun,
The fabric of togetherness, forever one.

Luminescence in Togetherness

In the glow of dusk, their spirits rise,
Shining brightly, like starlit skies.
Together they glow, in harmony's light,
Creating warmth that banishes night.

Through whispered hopes, they light the way,
Lending their hearts to guide each day.
In shared laughter, they spark the flame,
A luminescence, never the same.

With every smile, they spark a change,
Their radiance spreads, both bright and strange.
Together they shimmer, a cosmic dance,
In the light of love, they find their chance.

In unity's glow, they rise and shine,
Minds intertwined, their futures align.
For in the brilliance of what they share,
Lives a luminescence, beyond compare.

Resonance of Hidden Journeys

In silent footsteps, they roam unknown,
Winding paths where dreams have grown.
Through shadows they wander, hand in hand,
The resonance of journeys, perfectly planned.

Their spirits echo, through the dark,
Guided by whispers, igniting a spark.
In quiet moments, their stories blend,
Unveiling truths, as they transcend.

With each step forward, they unveil the light,
Hidden journeys come into sight.
Through trials faced and laughter shared,
They find a bond that's unprepared.

Together they rise, through every strife,
The resonance grows, reflecting their life.
In the heart's ledger, secrets entwine,
A testament to journeys, yours and mine.

Illuminated Paths Together

Underneath the vast, bright sky,
We walk where dreams like rivers flow.
Hand in hand, we never sigh,
For in this light, our spirits glow.

With every step, the shadows flee,
Guided by the stars above.
In every laugh, we are set free,
Each moment woven with our love.

Through valleys deep, on mountains high,
We carve our names in nature's grace.
With every glance, we learn to fly,
Two hearts entwined in time and space.

Together, we embrace the dawn,
As colors wash the world anew.
With hope like petals, gently drawn,
Our journey sings of me and you.

The Alchemy of Souls

In whispered dreams, our spirits meet,
A dance unfolds in twilight's glow.
With every heartbeat, love is sweet,
Transforming time, our magic flows.

Embers spark in twilight air,
Each glance a potion, pure and rare.
With every touch, the world feels right,
We craft our dreams from dark to light.

Together lost in endless night,
Bound by fate, our souls entwined.
From fleeting shadows, we ignite,
In this alchemy, we find the kind.

As stardust lingers, we ascend,
The universe, our canvas wide.
Through love's embrace, we'll always mend,
In every heartbeat, side by side.

Unseen Ties of the Heart

In silent whispers, hearts align,
Invisible threads weave through the air.
Though miles apart, a bond can shine,
In every pulse, we feel and care.

Connections bloom in secret nights,
With dreams that sail on hope's soft wings.
Through shadows deep, we find the lights,
As destiny, our song now sings.

Though words may falter, truth remains,
In every glance, a universe.
Through joy and sorrow, love sustains,
In every heartbeat, we immerse.

Together, we can face the storms,
For in our souls, we carry grace.
With unseen ties that keep us warm,
We find our place, our sacred space.

Mosaic of Mutual Truths

In fragments scattered, we unite,
Each piece reflects a story told.
With every voice, we find the light,
Our mosaic shines, in colors bold.

Through trials faced, we learn to stand,
In every struggle, truths emerge.
With open hearts, we join our hands,
Together strong, we find our urge.

In laughter shared and tears that fall,
We paint a picture, vast and grand.
From whispers soft to echoes tall,
Our stories bind, a sacred band.

As life unfolds, we bravely tread,
Each challenge faced, a step we take.
In unity, no fear nor dread,
A canvas rich, our hearts awake.

The Symphony of Us

In harmony we dance, so intertwined,
Melodies cascade, like stars aligned.
Every note a whisper, every glance a tune,
Together we create, 'neath the silver moon.

Hearts beat in rhythm, the world fades away,
Lost in the music, come what may.
With every crescendo, our spirits soar high,
A symphony eternal, you and I.

In the silence between, our souls gently speak,
In the calm of the night, our love feels unique.
As violins lead, our laughter rings true,
In this grand overture, it's all about you.

So let the world listen, we'll play on this stage,
In the symphony of us, we'll never age.
With every heartbeat, our story's penned,
A melody of love, that will never end.

Bridges Across Time

Underneath the stars, two hearts once met,
Crossing the rivers, no need to forget.
Bridges of memories, we carefully build,
As echoes of laughter, time's light is thrilled.

Woven through ages, our paths intertwine,
The past and the future, forever align.
With every step forward, the shadows retreat,
In the arms of our dreams, we're destined to meet.

Years may advance, yet the bond stays the same,
Each moment a spark, igniting the flame.
Through valleys and mountains, we'll journey as one,
With bridges of love, our souls will outrun.

So let's walk together, hand in hand, side by side,
Amongst the stars shining, our love is our guide.
Across every timeline, our hearts will abide,
On bridges of memories, eternally tied.

Woven Destinies

Threads of our lives, intricately spun,
In the fabric of time, we are never done.
With each gentle touch, a tapestry grows,
Woven destinies bloom, as the wind softly blows.

Colors collide, bright hues intertwine,
Patterns of laughter, our love is divine.
In the loom of the universe, patterns take flight,
Binding our spirits, in the stillness of night.

Every twist and turn, a story unfolds,
In the echo of silence, our hearts gently hold.
Through trials and trials, like threads we remain,
Linked by our dreams, through joy and through pain.

So let's embrace the weave, with gratitude true,
In this dance of existence, it's me and it's you.
Together we flourish, come what may,
In this tapestry of life, forever we'll stay.

Conversations in Silence

With eyes that convey what words cannot speak,
In moments of stillness, our hearts gently seek.
Whispers of feelings, in silence we share,
A language of love, floating softly in air.

Time pauses briefly, in the hush of the night,
As shadows of dreams envelop us tight.
Each heartbeat a question, each glance an embrace,
In the quiet of being, we find our own place.

Between breaths, a story, unspoken yet clear,
In the depth of connection, there's nothing to fear.
For in the tranquility, our spirits ignite,
Conversations of love, flickering light.

So let's linger awhile, in this peaceful retreat,
Where silence speaks volumes, where hearts gently meet.
In the beauty of quiet, our souls intertwine,
In conversations of silence, forever you're mine.

Harmony in Whispered Vows

In the twilight's gentle embrace,
Promises linger, soft and still.
Hearts entwined in a sacred space,
Feelings rise, a quiet thrill.

Beneath the stars, we share our dreams,
Fingers touch, a spark ignites.
Love flows like soft, flowing streams,
Binding our souls on peaceful nights.

Words unspoken find their way,
Echoes of what we cannot say.
In silence, our spirits sway,
A dance where time melts away.

Together we weave our fate,
In harmony, our voices blend.
Two souls meet, no room for wait,
Through whispered vows, our hearts transcend.

Threads of Understanding

In the fabric of our lives,
Each thread a moment, a shared tone.
Woven tightly, the heart strives,
To create a world of our own.

Colors blend in the light of day,
Patterns form, both bold and true.
With every challenge, come what may,
We find strength in what we do.

From distant shores, our paths align,
Two stories merge, a tapestry.
In the silence, love will shine,
As we build our legacy.

Hand in hand, we journey forth,
Through the storms and through the calm.
Each thread connects, its true worth,
In understanding, we find our balm.

The Dance of Kindred Spirits

Underneath the silver moon,
Two figures sway, a whispered tune.
In their movements, pure delight,
Kindred spirits, lost in night.

With every step, a story told,
Of laughter shared and hands to hold.
Time stands still, the world fades away,
In this dance, forever we stay.

Eyes locked tight, a silent vow,
In this moment, here and now.
With every beat, our hearts align,
In this rhythm, love will shine.

Together we twirl in perfect grace,
Finding solace in each embrace.
The dance will lead, there's no defeat,
For kindred souls will always meet.

Tapestry of Shared Dreams

In the quiet of the morning light,
We stitch our hopes, a gleam so bright.
Threads of gold, of blue and green,
Creating visions yet unseen.

With every thought, we cast the line,
For future paths where dreams entwine.
New colors fade and shadows form,
Yet in our hearts, we feel the warm.

We shape the fabric of our days,
As thoughts and wishes blend in rays.
Each whispered hope, a vibrant hue,
Together we've forged a world anew.

United in our quest for more,
We unlock every waiting door.
In this tapestry, hand in hand,
We weave our stories, bold and grand.

Tides of Mutual Understanding

In quiet whispers, secrets flow,
Like rivers winding, we both know.
An ebb and flow, our hearts entwined,
In this vast ocean, love defined.

With every wave, a story told,
Of laughter shared and hands to hold.
Through tempests fierce and calm so clear,
Together still, we have no fear.

Our bond, it deepens, like the sea,
Where depths of trust will always be.
In tidal pools, we find our place,
A dance of souls, a warm embrace.

As moonlight shines on waters blue,
In stillness, we find something new.
With every tide, our hearts align,
In love's true rhythm, we will shine.

A Garden of Shared Dreams

In a garden where blooms arise,
We plant our hopes 'neath sunny skies.
With every seed, a vision grows,
A tapestry of all that glows.

Butterflies dance on gentle breeze,
Whispers of love among the trees.
We nurture dreams, let blossoms spread,
In fragrant fields where paths are led.

Together, we tend to each flower,
With patience true, in every hour.
Through seasons' change, we'll hold our ground,
In shared tomorrows, joy is found.

With roots entwined, we stand so tall,
In this sweet garden, we shall not fall.
For in these blooms, we see our fate,
In love's embrace, we cultivate.

When Two Become One

In quiet moments, we align,
Two hearts beating, yours and mine.
A gentle touch, a knowing glance,
In this sweet world, we take our chance.

With every laugh, our spirits soar,
Together strong, we seek for more.
In every dream, our visions blend,
A bond so deep, we will transcend.

Through trials faced and joys embraced,
In your warm eyes, my fears erased.
Two souls entwined, a sacred dance,
In every heartbeat, love's advance.

With whispered vows that time won't sever,
We find our strength, now and forever.
In unity, we'll rise above,
For in this world, we are in love.

Melodies of Shared Moments

In laughter's song, our spirits sing,
With every note, a joy we bring.
The harmony of hearts combined,
In shared moments, love is defined.

As time unfolds, the music flows,
With each new day, our rhythm grows.
In whispers soft, our secrets blend,
In every measure, we transcend.

With melodies that fill the air,
In laughter's echo, we are bare.
Together strumming, hearts in tune,
Underneath a silver moon.

In every chord, a story plays,
Of simple joys and love's sweet gaze.
In life's grand symphony, we'll sway,
In perfect time, we find our way.

www.ingramcontent.com/pod-product-compliance
Ingram Content Group UK Ltd.
Pitfield, Milton Keynes, MK11 3LW, UK
UKHW020126171224
452675UK00014BA/1602